LIFELONG BIRD MIGRATION

Lebenslang Vogelzug

JÜRG AMANN
Translated from the German by Marc Vincenz

SPUYTEN DUYVIL
New York City

Publication of this volume is in part made possible by
ProHelvetia, the Swiss Arts Council.

prohelvetia

Jürg Amann: Lebenslang Vogelzug. Gedichte
© Haymon Verlag, Innsbruck-Wien 2014
Translation ©2017 Marc Vincenz
ISBN 978-1-944682-47-7

Library of Congress Cataloging-in-Publication Data

Names: Amann, Jèurg, 1947- author. | Vincenz, Marc, translator.
Title: Lifelong bird migrations : Lebenslang Vogelzug / Jèurg Amann ;
    translated from the German by Marc Vincenz.
Other titles: Lebenslang Vogelzug
Description: New York : Spuyten Duyvil, 2017. | Parallel texts in German and
    English.
Identifiers: LCCN 2017020475 | ISBN 9781944682477
Classification: LCC PT2661.M14 A6 2017 | DDC 831/.914--dc23
LC record available at https://lccn.loc.gov/2017020475

For Anna, my great love

Contents

To lie there as such,	3
peace	5
Morning by the Sea	7
yet another autumn	9
Late Autumn	11
A Spring Day in Winter	13
Winter Evening at Wannsee	15
Those noises	17
Again, the wall of fog.	19
Lifelong Bird Migration	21
If, how	23
Invocation	25
Prayer I	27
down deep below	29
how the hell should I put this?	31
Who, where	33
To raise the voice once more—	35
Heave	37
Prayer II	39
Remembrance	41
Reverb	43
Fragment	45
Never Ever	47
My mother	49
Haiku	51
Saying, Asking	53
A Few Sentences on Grief	55
Pain, the strain	57
Do you recall,	59

Prayer III	61
How far can I still	63
Love Song	65
Dreamt of love	67
Suddenly there	69
Still one more love	71
Last Questions	73
For A.	75
Lovers in Abeyance	77
Canticle Variation	79
Canticle Variation II	83
Cavafy Variation	85
While Reading Seferis	87
Traveling to Phoenix	89
Cretan Easter	91
To the Memory of Anita Pichler	93
Poem for the Madonna	97
Caduta d'Angeli	101
Happy Ice Age	103
Become Catholic again,	105
To learn from the trees,	107
The world changed:	109
Letter	111
Calm creeps in	113
Whence?	115
Time reads	117
Someone Like Hölderlin Walks	119
When	123
The Poem	125
Dream	127
Outside	129

LEBENSLANG
VOGELZUG

LIFELONG
BIRD MIGRATION

So daliegen, so
> mit geöffneten Sinnen, als ob
>> es schon das Skelett wäre.

Den Luftzug spüren,
> durch die geweiteten Augen.
Die Nähe des Steins.

To lie there, as such,
        senses wide open, as if
                already your own skeleton.

To feel that draft of wind
        through the widened eyes,
and the headstone's close proximity.

FRIEDEN

die stille
wenn der mensch aufhört.

der friedliche
kampf der tiere.

der aufstand
der zertretenen blumen.

PEACE

that silence
when humanity ceases.

the peaceful
rampage of young animals.

the uprising
of the trampled flowers.

Morgen am Meer

Und grosse Vögel gingen
durch das Rot des frühen Tags.
Des Bruders Frühgestalt.
Der Schlaf. Der Sonnen
Aufstand.

Morning by the Sea

And grotesque birds flocked
through that red glare of dawn.
Brother's early apparition.
Sleep. And then suddenly, the sun's
uprising.

WIEDER EIN HERBST

wieder ein herbst
als ob
es noch mehr davon gäbe.

ein spätlicht
als ob
es noch frühe.

das ist aber ein wunsch.
und die gewöhnung

YET ANOTHER AUTUMN

yet another autumn
as if
there were many more.

then that late light
as if
it were still morning.

but that is just a whim.
and an old habit

SPÄTHERBST

Das rote Haus wieder,
    dort drüben,
        wenn es das Licht fängt.

Das helle Braun der Blätter
    vor dem Blau des Sees.

Und grosse, mir ganz unbekannte
    Vögel.

Der Laubfall. Das Abtreiben
    der Blätter.

Und immer noch Boote.

Der Wind greift nicht mehr
    ins Geäst.
Die Zeit
    steht still.

Der Himmel
    lädt sich auf
        mit Blei.

Late Autumn

The red house, back
    over there again
        when it catches the light.

The bright brown of leaves
    against the blue tint of the lake.

And, utterly unknown to me,
    those strange burly birds.

A shedding. That drift
    of inconsequential leaves.

And boats are still moored.

The wind no longer grasps
    into the foliage, and
time stands
    untimely still.

The sky
    loads up
        with lead.

Frühlingstag im Winter

Ganz helle Horizonte. Venezianisches Licht.
Palast der Gebirge, geschichtet, getürmt.
Darunter, davor, zwischen den Hügeln und leuchtend,
Nebelbänder, über dem See.

Gelegentlich Rauch, darunter, darüber.
Die Wiesen noch braun.
Die Bäume noch schwarz und schmal.
Schatten wie von Giacometti
gehen durch andere Schatten hindurch.
Blasse Gesichter von Menschen,
die in die Sonne sehen.
Müde, gefältelte Haut. Ruhige Augen.
Und auch die Kinder noch still.

A Spring Day in Winter

Dappling horizons. Venetian light.
Stacked palace of mountain chains, layered.
And beneath, before and between the slopes, illuminating
ribbons of mist dancing over the lake.

An occasional wisp of smoke, beneath, above.
The fields are still brown.
The trees still black and minuscule,
and yet, Giacometti's illusive shadows
weave through other people's umbrage.
Pale faces of humans
staring deep into a sun.
Tired, creased skin and those tranquil eyes.
The children remain quite still.

WINTERABEND AM WANNSEE

Wieder nachtet es ein.
Und der Nebel steigt
aus den Wäldern.

Und der See trägt noch, westlich,
einen Anflug von Röte,
den Tag.

Und die Ferne, östlich, nimmt ab.
Wasser und Land verschwimmen.
Alles wird Himmel. Die Äste ragen,
weiss-schwarz, hinein.
Die Vögel fallen
zum Schlaf.

Winter Evening at Wannsee

Once again, it darkens.
Fog rises deep
out of the forests.

And westward, the lake still carries
that hint of blush:
lost day.

Eastward, distance diminishes.
A blur of water and land.
The branches push white-black holes
into the skin
of an expansive sky.
The birds fall
into sleep.

Die Geräusche,
dicht neben mir,
nachts.
Das Knacken,
wenn auf der schwarzen Fensterscheibe
die Eisblumen wachsen,
eine Kristallknospe aufspringt.
Am Morgen
wird man es sehen.

Those noises
closing in beside me
at night.
That crackling
when the frost-fern exhales
across a black windowpane,
a crystal bud snaps open.
In the morning
you will surely see it.

Wieder die Nebelwand.
Wieder am Abend. Wieder
das ferne Läuten der
Glocken in mir.

Aus Traumfurchen
wächst dunkel die Frucht.

Again, the wall of fog.
Again, in the evening. Again
that distant chiming
of bells within me.

A fear of dreaming
makes my fruit grow bitterly dark.

LEBENSLANG VOGELZUG

Und Vögel fliegen Zeichen
in die Luft. Ein Rauch
steigt auf. Das Licht
geht unter. Gruft.

Lifelong Bird Migration

And birds scrawl symbols
across the sky. A puff of smoke
rises. Light sinks
down into the deepening vault.

OB, WIE

Wenn man nur wüsste, wie
sie gemeint ist, die Welt.
Diese rollende Kugel,
in den Gnadenmantel
      aus blauem Himmel gehüllt.
Auf der es die Liebe gibt.

Und wir,
die wir sie einstweilen bewohnen.

Ob wir gemeint sind.
Ob sie gemeint ist, die Welt.

If, how

If we only knew, how
she was intended, our World.
This whirling ball
wrapped in a merciful
      blue-sky cloak
where love subsides.

And we, we
who inhabit her in our meantime.

If we are intended.
If she is intended, our World.

ANRUFUNG

Wir müssen wieder
die Dome bauen, den Gott
wieder anrufen, ihn an-
locken durch die Behausung
in unserer Mitte.

Invocation

We should build
the dome again,
invoke God again, en-
tice him through the abode
within our midst.

GEBET I

Aber auch aufgehen
kann uns der Gott wieder, aufstehen
am Rand, aus dem Zwielicht,
wo er unterging, einmal,
einging in seine Ewigkeit.
Warte

Prayer I

But God also can
rise for us again, stand
at the edge, emerge from the twilight
where he once sank,
plunged into his own eternity.
Just wait

tief hinab
    wo das urgestein wurzelt
        geht meine suche nach gott.

down deep below
>   where the bedrock is rooting
>   is my quest for god.

wie soll ich sagen?

einmal gestürzt ist die son-
ne auf mich herab.

how the hell should I put this?

once the sun came
crashing down upon me.

Wer, wo
      die Luft aufhört, hört,
          ausser uns, die Musik,
durch welche wir aber beten?

Who, where
      air ends, truly hears,
            besides us, the music
through which we pray?

Noch einmal die Stimme erheben,
     höher, weit
       über uns hinaus,
solange der Atem noch trägt.

To raise the voice once more—
    higher—far
      into the stratosphere,
as long as breath holds on.

Den Grabfelsen weg-
wälzen von den
Lippen und auf-
erstehen zur Sprache.

Heave
those gravestones
from the lips and re-
surrect the tongue.

Gebet II

Ich bin das Rätsel.
Löse mich.

Ich bin das Blatt am Baum.
Löse mich.

Ich bin das Gewölk
und der Nebel über dem Wasser.
Löse mich.

Amen.

Prayer II

I am my own puzzle.
Please release me.

I am the leaf on the tree.
Please release me.

I am the cloudbank
and that fog settling over the water.
Please release me.

Amen.

ERINNERUNG

Etwas wie ein Waldrücken.
Der mich trug,
als mich die Eltern nicht trugen.
Der Rücken des Rossbergs.

Remembrance

Something like the saddle of the forest
supported me
when my parents didn't:
that solid backbone of the Rossberg mountains.

Anklang

Mein Herz, sei ruhig
und schlafe; sieh, meines,
besänftigt, schläft auch.

Reverb

My heart, be still
and sleep; behold, my own,
soothed, sleeps too.

Fragment

Lass uns in die Felder fallen
wie der Abendwind.

Fragment

Let us fall into the pastures
like evening wind.

Nicht, nie

Nicht aufhören, nie,
mit nichts,
sagte der alte Mann,
sei sein Rezept
gegen den Tod
gewesen, immer.

Never Ever

Don't despair, never,
over anything,
said the old man.
His formula
to counter death,
always.

Meine Mutter
mit den geschlossenen Augen,
als ich zu spät kam,
um sie noch einmal zu sehen.

(Nach Friederike Mayröcker.
Vorstellung, unerträglich.)

My mother
with the closed eyes
when I came too late
to see her one more time.

(After Friederike Mayröcker.
Intolerable notion.)

HAIKU

nach und für Hertha Kräftner (1928–1951)

Sterben im Gehen
sterbend die Strasse sehen
– die weitergeht

Haiku

after and for Hertha Kräftner (1928–1951)

To die walking,
dying watching the street
—that goes on.

SAGEN, FRAGEN

Sterben werde ich
zwischen Daumen und Zeigefinger,
hat meine Mutter im Traum gesagt.

Ich bin nicht weit genug gegangen,
sagte der Grossvater,
als es zum Sterben kam.

Es ist grauenhaft, sagte der Vater,
als ich ihn drüben besuchte,
er meinte das Essen.

Was werden wir uns einmal gewesen sein,
von dort aus gesehen, fragte die Liebe,
nachdem sie gestorben war.

Aber ich dann, was frage ich,
was sage ich, von hüben und drüben,
wem, und in wessen Traum?

Sagen und Fragen.

Saying, Asking

I shall die
between thumb and forefinger,
my mother said in a dream.

I have not gone far enough,
said my grandfather
marching to his death.

It is awful, said my father
when I visited him over there.
He meant the food.

What will we have been to each other,
seen from over there, asked my love
after she had passed over.

And me? What should I ask
on either of these sides,
to whom, and in whose dream?

Saying and asking.

Sätze zur Trauer

Und eine Weile
trauert der Mensch.

Trauer
trägt das Haus,
die Läden bleiben
geschlossen.

Kommt wieder Trauer auf.

Ich habe Liebes
verloren.

So endet das Schöne.

A Few Sentences on Grief

And for a while
man grieves.

Grief,
the foundation of the house,
the shops remain
shuttered.

Then, grief rises again.

I have lost
a sense of love.

Beauty ends on that note.

Aus Leid
das Lied.

Pain, the strain
of the song.

Weisst du noch,
weisst du noch
in Venedig,
wie uns das Kind starb,
unter der Hand,

unter der Hand,
mit der wir uns
liebten, liebten
wir uns denn
nicht genug?

Do you recall,
do you recall
in Venice,
how our child died
on the quiet,

and how, on the quiet,
we loved
each other. Did we not
love each other
quite enough?

Gebet III

Ich möchte jetzt nahe bei dir
liegen. Meine Begrenzung eng an die deine
fügen. Neben dir leben und sterben
wie einer. Und meine Haut
nicht mehr retten vor deiner.

Prayer III

Right now I should like to lie down
beside you. Meld my limitations
with yours, live and die beside you
as one—and not to save my skin
from yours.

Wie weit kann ich noch
gehen, wie weit noch fort,
damit ich zurück bin,
bei dir, wenn die Erde
uns umwirft?

Ich möchte ja neben dir
liegen.

How far can I still
drift, how far to go away
to be back
at your side again when the Earth
capsizes us?

You know, I should like to lie
beside you.

LIEBESLIED

Stell dir vor, es wäre wirklich
zu Ende, das Licht
ginge ganz
aus oder an, weil
die Welt in die Sonne
fällt oder weg,
in den Schatten der Sterne.

Oder des Kriegs, und es würde
einen Augenblick lang ganz
still oder laut,
bevor der Aufschlag
ans Herz geht,
wir wären dann nicht
zusammen, um uns zu halten.

Love Song

Imagine it
ceased, the light
switched
off or on, because
the world tumbled into the Sun
or swirled away
into the stars' shadows.

Or because of war, and
for a split-second long
it would become
silent or loud
just before the impact
drove into the heart,
then we wouldn't be together
to embrace each other.

Wieder
von der Liebe geträumt
nachts aber
sie weinte

Dreamt of love
again
nights
she wept

Plötzlich steht da
wer
wieder die Frau
was
wieder die Liebe
wie
und was tut sie

Steht da
und
geht nahe

Suddenly there
who
that woman again
what
love again
how
and what does she do

She stands there
and
edges closer

Noch eine Liebe
zu wagen ...

Unter dem Zeichen
des Sturms?

Still one more love
to venture ...

Beneath the symbol
of the storm?

LETZTE FRAGEN
für A.

Bei wem möchte ich sein
am Ende? Wen halten? Wem
die Angst wegküssen? Wessen
Sterben mit dem eigenen Sterben
zudecken? Über wessen Tot-
sein gebeugt sein im Tod?

Paare,
die so entstehen.

Last Questions
for A.

With whom do I want to be
at the end? Embrace whom? Who
to kiss fear away with? Whose
death should be blanketed with my
own? And, to be hunched over whose lifeless-
ness in my own death?

Couples,
coming into being thus.

An A.

Alles ist leichter geworden,
seit ich dich kenne.
Das Aufstehen am Morgen
und das Zubettgehen am Abend.
Die Nächte, die Tage, dazwischen.
Das Schöne, das Schwere.
Der Schmerz über die Hanglage der Welt.
Über die Sturzbahn des Lebens.
Das Beten. Trotz allem oder erst recht.
Das Glauben, das Nichtglauben an Gott.
Nur das Sterben ist wieder schwerer geworden,
seit ich dich kenne.

For A.

Everything has become simpler
since I have known you.
Rising in the morning
and going to bed in the evening.
The nights, the days in between.
The beautiful, the burdens,
that anguish of a world on a slope.
The landslide of life.
The praying—despite everything or more than ever.
The faith or lack of ... in God.
Only dying has become more difficult
now that I know you.

DIE LIEBESRUHENDEN

Ich lag hinter ihr, an ihren Rücken geschmiegt, tief
in ihr drin, und sah über ihre Schulter hinweg, an der ich
mich festhielt, auf den kleinen Balkon hinaus und
hinter dem Balkongeländer auf den Hafen und auf die
Bucht; wir sprachen leise, wir wollten nicht gehört
werden in den angrenzenden Zimmern; wir hörten
Musik, Schumann: Es war, als hätt' der Himmel die
Erde still geküsst; manchmal bewegte ich mich ein
wenig in ihr; auf dem Flur ging eine Tür auf oder zu;
während draussen alle zwei Stunden die grossen
Fähren einliefen und ablegten, abwechslungsweise,
und sich entluden und füllten; die anschlagenden
Geräusche drangen zu uns herein, die stählernen
Schlunde öffneten und schlossen sich direkt vor uns;
der – zunehmende? – Mond hatte schon am
Nachmittag über dem Wasser gestanden, nun, in der
heraufwachsenden Nacht, vergoss er aus seinem
Feuchtigkeit verheissenden Hof sein stillmachendes
Licht über die Ölhaut des Meeres, über die Eisenhaut
der Schiffe, über unsere müde gewordene
Menschenhaut.

Lovers in Abeyance

I lay behind her nestled into her back, deep
inside her, and looked over her shoulder (which
I held on to) out on to the small balcony and
behind the railing and into the port and
the cove; we spoke quietly, we didn't want to be
heard in the adjacent rooms; we discerned
music, Schumann: it was as if the sky had kissed
the Earth into silence; sometimes I moved myself
a little within her; in the hallway doors opened, closed,
while outside, every two hours, the bulky
ferries alternately arrived and unloaded,
and loaded and filled, the hammering
noises encroaching upon us, their steely
throats opening and closing directly ahead;
the—waxing?—moon already hung
over the water in late afternoon, and now, the
swelling night, out of its forebodingly damp
halo, spilled a quieting light
over the oily skin of the sea, over the steel skin
of the vessels, over our exhausted
human surfaces.

HOHELIED-VARIATION
für A.

Lass uns hineingehn,
meine Geliebte,
nimm mich mit unter dein Dach,
lade mich ein
in dein Haus.
Ich bringe Speise und Trank.
Lass mich sie ausbreiten vor dir,
lass mich sie hinlegen
zu deinen Füssen,
lass mich sie anrichten für dich.

Schaue sie an, meine Geliebte,
mit deinen begehrlichen Augen,
schaue sie an und tue das Deine dazu.

Bücke dich,
bücke dich zu mir hinab,
lege es neben das Meine,
lege dich selber dazu.
Wir wollen nehmen von uns,
was uns gefällt.

CANTICLE VARIATION
for A.

Let us enter,
my love,
guide me under your roof,
invite me
into your abode.
I will bring victuals and libations.
Let me spread them before you,
let me lay them
at your toes,
let me serve them to you.

Look, my love,
with your ravenous eyes,
look at them and place yours here too.

Bend down,
bend down from above,
lay them next to mine,
and lay yourself down here too.
We should take from each other
at our pleasure.

Schau mich an, meine Geliebte,
schaue mich an und nimm.
Alles an mir ist dir.
Nimm es. Nimm von mir,
was dich freut.
Trink mich aus,
meine Geliebte,
trink und iss meinen Leib,
er ist dein.
Und lass mich nehmen
von deinem.

Look, my love,
look at me and partake.
Everything mine is yours.
Grasp it. Take of me
what pleases you.
Imbibe me,
my love,
drink and devour my body,
it belongs to you.
And let me partake
of yours too.

HOHELIED-VARIATION II
für A.

Lass deine Kleider fallen, Geliebte.
Führe mich in den Wald.
Führe mich zu der Lichtung
in seiner Mitte.
Führe mich an den Teich.
Nimm dein Tier bei der Hand
und führ es zur Tränke.
Und wenn sein Durst gestillt ist,
stille ihn auch.

Dann erst, Geliebte,
wenn du und ich still sind,
wenn wir gestillt sind,
wenn alles am Teich still ist,
dann lass es Nacht werden
über dem Wald.
Dann zieh dein Kleid wieder an.

Canticle Variation II
for A.

Drop your clothes, my love.
Lead me into the woods,
to the clearing
at its center.
Lead me to the pond.
Take your creature by the hand
and guide him to the watering hole.
and when his thirst is quenched,
quiet him also.

Only then, my love
when you and I are still,
when we have become stilled,
when all at the pond is quiet,
let the night
close over the woods
and slip your dress back on.

KAVAFIS-VARIATION
für A.

An Ithaka immer vorbei
nimm deine Fahrt,
solange es geht,
solange du Wind
in den Segeln hast,
solang du die Richtung
selber bestimmst;

immer ins Offene,
immer zum Horizont,
über den Horizont
hinaus, fürchte das offene
Meer nicht, der Horizont
fährt mit, der Horizont
ist Rand genug, rundum,
und Poseidon begegnet
dir im Sturm nicht;

nicht ans Ufer,
nicht ans Gestade,
nicht auf das feste Land
setze aus freien Stücken
den Fuss, da, wo du herkommst,
kommst du noch früh genug
hin.

Cavafy Variation
for A.

Always pass Ithaca
on your travels,
as long as possible
as long as there is wind
in your sails,
as long as you can determine
the direction of your own free will;

always out into the open,
always toward the horizon,
then over the horizon
and beyond, do not fear
the open sea, the horizon
travels with you, the horizon
is enough of an edge all around,
and Poseidon will not meet you
with his storms;

not on the docks,
or on the shore,
not on solid ground,
plant your feet of your own
free will—there, from where you have come,
you will arrive soon
enough.

SEFERIS LESEND

Am Karfi,
unter dem einsamen Apfelbaum,
mit dem Rücken am Stamm,
auf der Erde, was
warst du da? Hirte?
Ohne Stock, ohne Herde?
Hirte der Welt, Hirte
für Frau und für Kind?

While Reading Seferis

There, in Karphi,
under that lone apple tree, leaning
your back against the trunk,
on the ground—what
were you there? A shepherd?
without a crook, without a herd?
Were you Shepherd of the world, Shepherd
of woman and of child?

REISE NACH PHÖNIX

Es ist immer hinter der Bucht
eine weitere Bucht, schöner als
diese, mit weisseren Steinen,
mit klareren Wassern, mit
einer Biegung, die weiter heran
an die Klippe reicht, an der sich
Himmel und Erde brechen.

Die so weit vor uns
in unserem Rücken zurückliegt,
dass wir uns schon an die kommende
nicht mehr erinnern.

Traveling to Phoenix

Behind this cove is always
another, more sublime than
this one, with white pebbles
and the clearest water, on
a curve that eventually
reaches the crag where
sky and earth split apart.

Yet that lies so far ahead,
behind our backs—
we no longer still recall
what is still to befall.

KRETISCHE OSTERN

Auch unter solcher Sonne ist Tod.
Seit Tagen hängt, gehäutet,
das Lamm unterm Baum.
Am Baum hängt der Jud.
Alles Blut in die Erde.
Nachts wird man ihn opfern.
Ans Kreuz mit ihm. Auge um Auge.
Auch aus der Kirche falscher Gesang.
Bratenduft in der Luft. Dreifach bekreuzigt.
Von Auferstehung auch hier keine Spur.

CRETAN EASTER

Even under *this* sun Death exists.
Hanged for days, skinned,
a lamb beneath the tree.
The Jew hangs in there,
all his blood drained into the soil.
At night he will be sacrificed.
Up on the cross with him. Eye for an eye.
Even from the church with its off-key song,
there's an aroma of roasted meat in the air. Thrice crucified,
and of resurrection not an inkling.

In memoriam Anita Pichler

Venedig. Im Winter. Nacht.
Kalt. Kalt auch in uns,
wie ihr toter Landsmann
gesagt hätte, als er noch lebte.
Sie lebt noch. Wir
leben noch. Gerade. Am Rand.
Riva degli Schiavoni. Wir sind
am Ende. Wir wissen
nicht weiter. Wissen nicht
weiter, was gilt.

Da tritt sie
aus dem Nebel, aus der vagen Linie
des Rands, aus dem Wasser,
an dem wir jetzt nah wohnen,
kommt auf uns zu, tritt,
vom Ende her, auf uns zu, schüttelt
das Wasser, den Nebel, das Ende, den Rand
aus ihrem schwarzen, aus ihrem grauen
Haar, sagt: Hallo, ich
will euch nicht stören, stört, ich
will euch nur grüssen, grüsst,
grüsst uns, stört uns zum Glück, schüttelt

To the Memory of Anita Pichler

Venice in winter. Nighttime.
Cold. Chill also within us,
just as her dead compatriot
had said when he still lived.
She *is* still living. And we
still survive—just about, on the edge.
Riva degli Schiavoni. We are at
our wit's end. How to
move on. We haven't a clue
how to, or what's really true.

Now she steps
out of the mist, from that vague border
on the edge, from the water
where we now reside near.
She comes toward us, walks
from the very end, shakes off
water, mist, the end itself, and the edge
from her black, her grey
hair, says: *Hello, I
don't want to disturb you* (but disturbs). *I
only wanted to say hello* (says hello), greets,
greets us, disturbs us (luckily), shakes

uns nur die Hand, bleibt nicht,
bleibt nicht bei uns, bleibt
nicht bei uns stehen, geht
weiter, ist weg, ist schon
fort. Aber wir
sind noch da, aber wir
sind noch da und dort.

our hands, doesn't stay,
doesn't remain, doesn't
stand by us, moves
on, is gone, is already
away. But we, we
remain, but we, we
remain here and there.

MADONNENGEDICHT
der Stadt Rottweil, zum Dank

Die Madonna habe noch kein Gedicht,
höre ich,
die von der Kapellenkirche,
die von der hinteren Seite,
die auf der Aussenwand,
die auf der Rückwand,
die sehr dunkle, sehr alte,
die den Müll der Geschichte,
und nicht nur den der Geschichte,
hat unter sich ergehen lassen müssen,
nicht über sich, unter sich,
wie der Stadtarchivar sagt,
die auf dem Mond steht,
auf der Nacht-, auf der Dunkelseite
der Welt,
auf seinem Sichelgesicht,
die ihr Kind davon weghebt,
hinan, nicht hinab,
da, wo sonst alles hingeht,
in den Orkus, den Bach hinunter,
nein hinauf, an den Bildhimmel,
den Steinhimmel, den Spitzbogen

POEM FOR THE MADONNA
with thanks to the city of Rottweil

The Madonna still doesn't have a poem,
I hear—
of the chapel church,
of the far side,
of the outside wall,
of the facing wall,
of the very dark, very ancient
leftovers of history,
and not just the history—
she had to let it wash away,
not over, but below her,
just as the city archivist says,
she who stands on the moon,
on the night- and the dark-side
of the world,
on its sickle face
that carried the child away,
upward, not downward,
where everything normally swirls
down into the underworld, down the tubes,
not upward toward the picturesque sky,
the starry sky, the pointed arch

des Bilddachs, des Bildstocks,
und meine Vorfahren kommen mir
in den Sinn,
die aus dem süddeutschen Raum,
die hier Steinmetze waren
oder gewesen sein sollen,
und jene andere Maria, jene Marie A.,
die vielleicht mit mir verwandt ist,
die über einem anderen Steinmetz
stand oder lag, über einem anderen Dichter,
hinauf also alles,
und nur ihr Blick geht hinab zu mir,
der Blick aus ihrem lichten Gesicht,
ein Gesicht, aber kein Gedicht,
denke ich, wie meine tote Mutter,
die auch noch kein Gedicht hat,
ein Buch, aber kein Gedicht,
sie ist so schön und ungeheuer oben,
wie meine Mutter,

sie hatten beide noch kein Gedicht,
jetzt haben sie eines.

of the cupola and the shrine—
and my ancestors come
to mind,
those from the southern-German realm,
who were stonemasons
or should have been,
and that other Maria, that Maria A.,
who is likely related to me,
who stood or lay beneath
another mason, above another poet—
everything was upward
and only her glance veers down toward me,
that glance from her eroded face,
visage but not verse,
I think—just like my dead mother,
who doesn't yet have a poem,
a book, but no poem,
and she is so beautiful and breathtaking up there,
just like my mother,

neither of them had a poem,
but now they both do.

CADUTA D'ANGELI

Attenzione, Caduta d'Angeli,
stand auf dem Schild
vor der venezianischen Kirche,
einer von hundertsechzig,
wie ich mich zu erinnern glaube,
Engelschlag wie anderswo Steinschlag,
Schlag auf Schlag jedenfalls,
von Kirchturm zu Kirchturm,
im Schlagschatten der Zeit,
folge ich meinem Herzschlag,
Schlag für Schlag,
bis ich hinschlage, schlagartig,
Herzschlag, Glockenschlag, Steinschlag,
gefallener Engel,
von einem Schlag auf den andern.

Caduta d'Angeli

Attenzione, Caduta d'Angeli,*
was written on the sign
in front of the Venetian church,
one of a hundred and sixty
as I seem to recall,
the fall of angels as elsewhere was rockfall,
either way, a falling upon a falling
from church tower to church tower,
shadows falling in time—
I follow my own footfall,
footfall upon footfall,
until even I fall over, in shortfall,
footfall, rainfall, rockfall.
Angels falling
from one moment to another.

*translation: *Caution: falling angels*

Fröhliche Eiszeit

Fröhliche Eiszeit
stand auf dem Plakat am Kiosk
an der Berliner Mauer,
westseits,
beim Brandenburger Tor,
am Besichtigungspunkt,
da wo Kennedy
zum Berliner geworden war,
vor dem Eisernen Vorhang,
und darunter, neben dem Bild
der verschiedenen Eissorten,
stand der Name
der Eisherstellerfirma.

Die Berliner Mauer ist abgetragen,
das Brandenburger Tor ist geöffnet,
der Eiserne Vorhang ist weg.

Die Eiszeit geht weiter.

Happy Ice Age

Happy Ice Age
was scrawled on the placard at the kiosk
at the Berlin wall,
on the Western side,
at the Brandenburg Arch,
at that sightseeing spot
where Kennedy
became a Berliner,
in front of the iron curtain;
and beneath, next to the picture
of assorted ice cream cakes
was the name
of a certain ice cream manufacturer.

The Berlin wall has been carted off in pieces,
the Brandenburg Arch is open for business,
the iron curtain vanished.

Yet the Ice Age continues.

Wieder katholisch werden,
wie Thomas Bernhard gesagt hat,
wieder katholisch werden im Alter,
oder wahnsinnig,
das ist die Wahl.

Become Catholic again,
as Thomas Bernhard had said,
become Catholic again in old age,
or completely insane,
that is the choice.

Von den Bäumen zu lernen:
nur dastehn und sein
—und unmerklich wachsen

To learn from the trees,
just stand there and be
—and grow imperceptibly.

Die Welt verändert:
Steine ins Wasser gelegt,
ein Stück Berg ins Meer.

The world changed:
rocks placed in the water became
a fragment of mountain in the ocean.

Brief

Lieber D.

Du immer wo
anders
nun also dort

ich hier
also fort
also da
wo auch schon
besser
was?
schreiben?
geschrieben gelebt

Dein J.

Letter

Dear D.

You always else-
where
now also over there

I here
well, gone
well, over there
where could be
better
right?
write?
lived written.

Yours, J.

Ruhe kehrt ein
nach dem Sturm.
Nicht vorher. Die Ruhe
vor dem Sturm
haben wir gar nicht
gehört.

Calm creeps in
after the storm.
Not before. The calm
before the storm
we never
heard coming.

Von wo?

Woher kommt der Tod?
Von oben oder von unten?
Von links oder von rechts?
Von aussen oder von innen?
Er kommt nicht. Wir kommen.

Whence?

Whence does death come?
Above or below?
Right or left?
From outside or inside?
He's not coming. We are.

Die Zeit liest
buchstabengenau.
Sie findet den verborgenen Sinn
in dem, was wir schreiben.

Time reads
to the letter.
It finds the hidden meaning
in what we write.

Einer wie Hölderlin geht

Einer wie Hölderlin geht von Nürtingen nach
Bordeaux
und wieder zurück.
Einer wie Hölderlin geht von Homburg nach
Frankfurt
und wieder zurück.
Einer wie Hölderlin geht von Homburg nach
Tübingen
und nicht mehr zurück.

Einer wie Lenz geht durchs Gebirg.

Einer wie Lenz geht von Strassburg nach Sesenheim
und wieder zurück.
Einer wie Lenz geht von Zürich nach Waldersbach
und wieder zurück.
Einer wie Lenz geht von Riga nach Moskau
und nicht mehr zurück.

Einer wie Wezel geht nicht mehr weiter.

Someone Like Hölderlin Walks

Someone like Hölderlin[1] walks from Nürtingen to
Bordeaux
and back again.
Someone like Hölderlin walks from Homburg to
Frankfurt
and back again.
Someone like Hölderlin walks from Homburg to
Tübingen
and doesn't return.

Someone like Lenz[2] walks across the mountains.

Someone like Lenz walks from Strasbourg to Sesenheim
and back again.
Someone like Lenz walks from Zurich to Walderbach
and back again.
Someone like Lenz walks from Riga to Moscow
and doesn't return.

Someone like Wezel[3] doesn't walk any further. Eine wie die

---

1 Johann Christian Friedrich Hölderlin (1770–1843) a major German lyric poet associated with Romanticism

2 Siegfried Lenz (1926–2014), a German writer of novels, short stories and essays

3 Johann Karl Wezel (1747–1819), German poet and author

Kräftner geht von Mattersburg nach
Wien
und nicht mehr zurück.
Einer wie Kleist geht an den Wannsee
und nicht mehr zurück.
Einer wie Walser geht nach Herisau
und nicht mehr zurück.

Einer wie Boehlendorff geht verloren.
Einer wie Heim geht aufs Eis.
Einer wie Burger geht durch die Wasserfallfinsternis
von Bad Gastein
und nicht mehr zurück.

Einer wie Hölderlin geht.

Someone like Kräftner[4] walks from Mattersburg to Vienna
and doesn't return.
Someone like Kleist[5] walks to the Wannsee
and doesn't return.
Someone like Walser[6] walks to Herisau
and doesn't return.

Someone like Boehlendorff[7] goes astray.
Someone like Heim[8] walks on ice.
Someone like Burger[9] walks through the Waterfall-Eclipse
of Badgastein
and doesn't return.

Someone like Hölderlin walks.

---

4 Hertha Kräftner (1928–1951) was an Austrian poet and diarist

5 Bernd Heinrich Wilhelm von Kleist (1777–1811) was a German poet, fiction writer and playwright

6 Robert Walser (1878–1956), Swiss, German-language poet, fiction writer–admired by Kafka

7 Casimir Ulrich Karl Boehlendorff (1775–1827), a Lithuanian, German-language poet and fiction writer

8 Peter Heim (1924—), German novelist

9 Hermann Burger (1942–1989), Swiss poet, essayist and fiction writer

WENN

Wenn ich gehe, gehe
ich plötzlich, und ich
sage es niemandem, nicht
einmal dir, denn du
würdest mich halten.

When

When I walk, I walk
all of a sudden, and I
tell no one, not
even you, because you
would hold me here.

Das Gedicht

Es sind jetzt sehr nahe zusammen
der Himmel und das Wasser,
die Kugel in den Kopf
und die Höhlen der Liebe;
über Leben und Sterben
entscheidet ein einziger Klang,
ein Reim in einem Gedicht;
und wäre es nicht,
in seinem dünnen Gelingen,
man wäre schon lange gegangen.

The Poem

Now they are very close,
the sky and the water,
that bullet in the head
and the caverns of love;
a single tone,
a rhyme in a poem decides
on life and death;
and were it not—
due to his dim successes—
one would have left long ago.

Traum

Im Traum verirrte ich mich.
Ich fand den Rückweg nicht mehr
zu den offenen Augen.
Jemand hatte sie mir zugedrückt.
Ich war tot.

Dream

In my dream, I went astray.
I could no longer find the way home
to my opened eyes.
Someone held them shut.
I was completely dead.

HINAUS

wenn der schnee wieder käme
in diese landschaft die
mich umzingelt
mit ihren aussichtspunkten
von denen herab ich
meine aussichten
betrachte vielleicht
dass ich durch ihn hindurch
meine spur wieder fände
hinaus

Outside

if the snow were to return
to this landscape that
encircles me
with its scenic overlooks
from whose heights
I might observe
my outlook
through which I might once again find
those tracks of mine leading
outside

About the Poet

Born in 1947, the son of a printer and poet, Jurg Amann attended high school in Winterthur and studied German literature at the University of Zurich and the Freie Universität Berlin. For many years he worked as a journalist and editor in Berlin, then later in Zurich. Amann was a poet, novelist, essayist, literary critic, dramatist and children's author. His prodigious oeuvre spans well over 40 literary works. He won many awards, including the Ingeborg Bachmann and Conrad-Ferdinand-Meyer prizes and two awards from the Swiss Schiller Foundation. He died in 2013.

About the Translator

Marc Vincenz is British-Swiss and the author of nine books of poetry and a novella. His latest are *This Wasted Land and Its Chymical Illuminations* (annotated by Tom Bradley) (Lavender Ink, 2015), *Becoming the Sound of Bees* (Ampersand Books, 2015) and *Sibylline* (Ampersand Books, 2016), and the novella, *Three Taos of T'ao, or How to Catch a White Elephant* (Spuyten Duyvil, 2017). Vincenz is also the translator of many German-language poets, including Herman Hesse Prize winner Klaus Merz, Werner Lutz, Erika Burkart, Alexander Xaver Gwerder, Andreas Neeser and Jürg Amann. Recent translations include *Out of the Dust* (Spuyten Duyvil, 2014) by Klaus Merz, *A Late Recognition of the Signs* (Spuyten Duyvil, 2015) and *Secret Letter* (Cervena Barva Press, 2016) both by Erica Burkart. His translation of Klaus Merz's *Unexpected Development* was a finalist in the 2016 Cliff Becker Prize for Translation and will be released by White Pine Press in 2018. He has received several grants from the Swiss Arts Council and a fellowship from the Literarisches Colloquium Berlin. His own work has been translated into many languages.